ART MASTERPIECES
IN 3-D

40 Images by Vermeer, Rembrandt, Goya,
and Other Great Artists

Image Selection and Text by L. C. Casterline

**BARNES
& NOBLE**

NEW YORK

Cover Images:

A Young Woman Seated at a Virginal, by Johannes Vermeer (front)

Ducal Palace and the Plaza of Saint Mark's (detail), by Canaletto (back)

Image credits on page 93

Designed by Iram Khandwala and Catherine Leonardo

Images converted to stereo by Tim McCulloch and Ryan Paola at the MAGroup, Bethel, CT

2006 Barnes & Noble Publishing

ISBN-13: 978-0-7607-8459-4

ISBN-10: 0-7607-8459-0

Printed and bound in China

1 3 5 7 9 10 8 6 4 2

INTRODUCTION

Throughout time, artists all over the world have created masterpieces in painting, sculpture, architecture, and more recently, in photography, collage, assemblage, and other media. The masterpieces in this book, however, are all paintings by European artists, many of whom are known as "Old Masters." The first group of these artists lived and worked during a period of intense

During the Renaissance, Italy consisted of the Kingdom of Two Sicilies in the South and independent city-states and republics in the north.

cultural activity in Europe called the Renaissance, which lasted from about 1400 to 1650.

In earlier times, painters and sculptors were in the same social class as other artisans, such as goldsmiths, tailors, or shoemakers, and few artists received credit for their work. Only during the Renaissance did artists start to gain recognition for their individual achievements and experience a rise in social status. Some artists were even elevated to the nobility.

The Renaissance was a time of great change. Many cities grew rich as centers of trade. Merchant ships established new trade routes around Africa to Asia, while Columbus sailed across the Atlantic, bringing back news of lands previously unknown to Europeans. Political power moved from the landowning aristocracy to wealthy merchant families, such as the de Médicis in Florence. These families expanded patronage of the arts beyond the Roman Catholic Church.

A new mindset among intellectuals also contributed to the burst of creativity during the Renaissance. In the 1300s, writers, such as Francesco Petrarch, and their followers had begun to rediscover the art, literature, and history of ancient Rome and Greece. As a result of their studies, humanists came to believe in a separation of church (spiritual matters) and state (civic matters), a well-rounded education (at least for their own class), and the worth of the individual.

The invention of the printing press in the mid-1400s resulted in the dissemination of many more books, easier circulation of ideas, and an increase in literacy. Illustrations were needed for the new books, which meant more and better printmakers. Among them were Albrecht Dürer and

In Germany, Albrecht Dürer became a master printmaker and book illustrator. His skill in making woodcuts is obvious in this print of *The Four Horsemen of the Apocalypse*.

Lucas Cranach the Elder, both friends of Martin Luther, whose challenge to the Roman Catholic Church resulted in the Reformation and the establishment of new Christian religions.

In the Netherlands, artists began using oil-based paints instead of tempera. Oils produced richer colors and could be applied to the surface in a number of ways, from a thin glaze to a thick impasto. Because oil paints were slower to dry, artists could rework their paintings, making corrections or changes as they pleased. Throughout Europe, oils would become the medium of choice for painters. In Florence, Filippo Brunelleschi, a sculptor and architect, developed linear perspective, a geometric and, therefore, scientific method of creating the illusion of three-dimensional space on a two-dimensional surface.

Pietro Perugino used linear perspective in creating his painting *Christ Handing the Keys to Saint Peter.*

The High Renaissance, from 1495 to 1520, was a period of unprecedented creative activity, particularly in Italy. During this time, Leonardo da Vinci, Michelangelo Buonarotti, and Raphael all worked in Florence. Leonardo was a true Renaissance man, working in the visual

Self-portrait of Leonardo da Vinci

arts, architecture, music, science, and engineering. In painting, he developed the techniques of chiaroscuro (the use of light and shade instead of line to model figures) and sfumato (very fine shading), and created some of the first modern scientific illustrations. Michelangelo carved some of the world's most expressive, lifelike sculptures and created the amazing frescoes on the ceiling of the Sistine Chapel in Rome. Raphael's paintings combined his own brilliant compositions with aspects of Leonardo's and Michelangelo's styles.

After the Renaissance, a new art style called Baroque came into favor. The style first appeared in Rome but would spread not only throughout Europe, but also to the new European colonies in the Americas and Asia. Baroque might be described as a style of excess.

Baroque paintings, such as those by Peter Paul Rubens, were filled with movement and color, while the outsize palaces, churches, and other buildings were covered with decoration inside and out. Artists also had more subjects to work with as landscapes, still-lifes, and genre pictures showing ordinary people engaged in everyday life became more popular.

In France, the aristocracy favored the lighthearted Rococo style, a celebration of love and fantasy exemplified by paintings such as Jean-Honoré Fragonard's *The Swing*. During this period, Marie-Louise-Élisabeth Vigée Lebrun made her mark as one of the most accomplished and successful portrait artists then practicing. She was one of the first two women admitted to the Royal Academy in Paris.

Romanticism reigned from the late 1700s to the mid-1800s. Among the artists associated with the Romantic style were J. M. W. Turner in England, Francisco Goya in Spain, and Jean-Baptiste-Camille Corot in France. No matter what their style, the Old Masters were remarkable both for the level of their creativity and for their consummate technical skill.

The Baroque architectural style can be seen in Venice's Santa Maria della Salute, designed by Baldassare Longhena.

Usually the type of 3-D effect used in this book is created with a stereo camera, which has two lenses set no more than 2.5 inches apart. This allows the photographer to take two photos at a time, each from a slightly different perspective. When the photographs are viewed through special lenses, the brain combines the two images into one 3-D image.

Art Masterpieces in 3-D, however, was made with photographs that already existed. To turn the images into stereo pairs, computer programs were used to separate each image into as many as 12 layers. Then each layer was examined to see which ones would work together to make the best 3-D image.

THE IMAGES

1430-1435
Tempera on wood
Museo del Prado, Madrid

The Annunciation (central panel)
Fra Angelico (ca. 1400–1455)

It's not certain from whom Fra Angelico (originally Guido di Pietro) received his artistic instruction, but he was probably first trained as a manuscript illuminator. Between 1419 and 1422, he entered the Dominican monastery of Santo Domingo de Fiesole in Tuscany. There he painted *The Annunciation* as an altarpiece for the monastery church. In the foreground, the archangel Gabriel tells Mary she will become the mother of Christ, who will redeem the sins of mankind, which are represented by the expulsion of Adam and Eve from the Garden of Eden in the background at left. The Holy Spirit is represented by a dove descending from God's hands in the upper left corner of the painting.

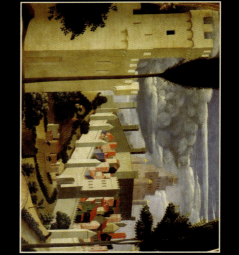

1435
Tempera on wood
Museo di San Marco, Florence

Deposition of Christ (detail)
Fra Angelico (ca. 1400–1455)

Fra Angelico took over the painting of *Deposition of Christ* from the artist Lorenzo Monaco, who had only completed the framework of three arches when he died. The detail shown here is from the background Fra Angelico painted in the top left-hand arch and pictures Jerusalem as a town in Tuscany. During his lifetime, Fra Angelico was known as Fra Giovanni, the name he took when he joined the Dominicans. After his death, he was called *pictor angelicus*, the angelic painter, which later became Fra Angelico. He was beatified by Pope John Paul II in 1984 and declared the patron of artists.

ca. 1485
Tempera on panel
Galleria degli Uffizi, Florence

The Birth of Venus (detail)
Sandro Botticelli (1445–1510)

Sandro Botticelli was born Alessandro di Mariano Filipepi in the Republic of Florence. Apparently the name Botticelli, which means "little barrel," was first given to Sandro's oldest brother, Giovanni, possibly because of his size, but later became the family name. By 1470, Botticelli had his own workshop in Florence. A favorite among the Médicis and other distinguished Florentine families, Botticelli was kept busy. His most famous painting, *The Birth of Venus*, was probably commissioned by a member of the Médici family. The painting illustrates Venus, standing on a clamshell, being blown ashore by Zephyr, god of the west wind, and Aura, goddess of the breeze. On the right, the goddess of spring (not shown) holds out a robe for Venus.

ca. 1489–1490
Tempera on wood panel
Galleria degli Uffizi, Florence

The Annunciation
Sandro Botticelli (1445–1510)

Sandro Botticelli painted many works with religious themes. In fact, in 1481, he was summoned to the republic of Rome by Pope Sixtus IV to paint frescoes on the walls of the Sistine Chapel along with several other distinguished artists. *The Annunciation* was commissioned for the convent of Cestello in Florence. The graceful movements of the archangel Gabriel and Mary and the billowing folds of their garments contrast with the orderly perspective of the floor tiles leading to the landscape in the background. Toward the end of Botticelli's life, his style of painting went out of fashion and he received few commissions. It was only in the late 1800s that his work came back into favor, gaining him new fame.

490–1500
Oil on wood
Musée du Louvre, Paris

The Ship of Fools
Hieronymus Bosch (ca. 1450–1516)

Hieronymus Bosch probably learned to paint at the family workshop in his native city of 's-Hertogenbosch, the Netherlands. He is considered one of the most imaginative painters of his time. *The Ship of Fools* is a fragment from a side panel of a triptych. It pictures several people, including a monk and two nuns, crowded into a small boat. In the foreground are two swimmers. Some historians believe the painting was inspired by Sebastian Brant's popular 1494 poem of the same title (in German, *Das Narrenschiff*), which chronicles the vices of over a hundred people sailing to a fool's paradise. Others think the painting is simply Bosch's vision of the folly of humankind. A third interpretation has it that Bosch painted the work as a commentary on corruption in the Catholic Church.

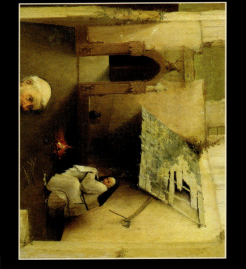

ca. 1510
Oil on wood
Museo del Prado, Madrid

The Bronchorst Bosschuyse Triptych (left panel, detail)
Hieronymus Bosch (ca. 1450–1516)

Hieronymus Bosch is best known for his fantastical paintings, such as *The Garden of Earthly Delights*, which pictures hundreds of naked people frolicking in an outdoor scene filled with strange structures, giant fruit, all kinds of animals, and beings that are half-human, half-creature. Strange paintings for a conservative Roman Catholic, perhaps, but Bosch also painted altarpieces and designed stained glass windows for the Church. *The Bronchorst Bosschuyse Triptych* was painted as an altarpiece. The central panel shows the Adoration of the Magi, while the side panels feature the donors of the piece. The detail shown is from the background of the left panel. Pictured is Saint Joseph sitting by a fire outside the ruins of King David's palace. The head in the foreground belongs to Saint Peter, who is standing behind the kneeling donor (not shown).

1496-1498
Woodcut
Museo Correr, Venice

Saint John Beholding the Seven Candelabra
Albrecht Dürer (1471–1528)

Albrecht Dürer's first artistic training was in the Nuremberg workshop of his father, a goldsmith. At age 15, already an accomplished draftsman, Dürer studied the art of making woodcuts and engravings. In the early 1490s, he traveled to northern Europe, including Switzerland, where he created woodcuts for Sebastian Brant's poem *Das Narrenschiff* (*The Ship of Fools*), which may have inspired Hieronymus Bosch's painting of the same name. Dürer also traveled to Italy and from 1495 on, his work incorporated elements of the Italian High Renaissance style. As the year 1500 approached, fears of the end of the world ran rampant, and Dürer, by now a master printmaker, produced his Apocalypse series. *Saint John Beholding the Seven Candelabra* illustrates Revelation 1: "I saw seven golden candlesticks; And in [their] midst . . . one like unto the Son of man. . . . his eyes were as a flame of fire . . . And he had in his right hand seven stars: and out of his mouth went a sharp two-edged sword: and his countenance was as the sun shineth in his strength."

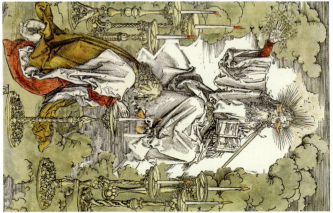

ca. 1525
Oil on wood
The National Gallery, London

Cupid Complaining to Venus
Lucas Cranach the Elder (1472–1553)

Lucas Cranach the Elder probably learned to paint from his father, who was also an artist. In 1505, Cranach was appointed court painter of Saxony by Friedrich the Wise, the founder of Wittenberg University and the protector of Martin Luther during the Reformation. In Wittenberg, Cranach became good friends with Luther and created the woodcut illustrations for his translation of the New Testament. As court painter, Cranach produced many portraits, and some believe he was the first artist to paint full-length portraits as stand-alone works of art. He also painted sensuous nudes in mythological settings. The painting shown here pictures Cupid complaining to Venus about being stung by bees while stealing honey.

ca. 1503–1505
Tempera on panel
Galleria degli Uffizi, Florence

The Holy Family

Michelangelo Buonarroti (1475–1564)

When 13-year-old Michelangelo announced his intention of becoming an artist, his father, a minor Florentine nobleman, was opposed. (Later, Michelangelo would write that his father thought artists were common laborers on a par with shoemakers.) Luckily, Michelangelo prevailed, as he went on to become one of the greatest sculptors of all time. He was also a master draftsman and painter, architect, and poet. *The Holy Family* was painted around the same time Michelangelo was finishing one of his most famous sculptures, the monumental *David*, and only a few years before he began work on the remarkable frescoes that illuminate the ceiling of the Sistine Chapel in Rome. In the painting, Mary is reaching back over her shoulder to take the Christ child from Joseph. The background figures represent the pagan world, while a young Saint John (at right) represents baptism, the way to move from paganism to Christianity.

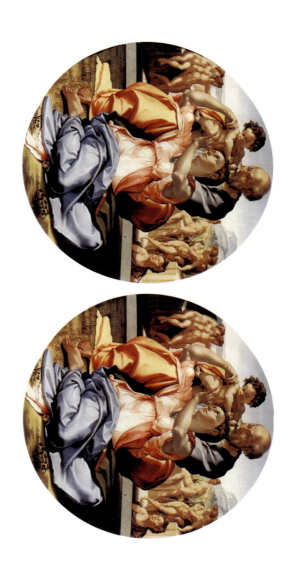

ca. 1522
Oil on panel
Galleria Borghese, Rome

The Incredulity of Saint Thomas
Ludovico Mazzolino (ca. 1480–d. after 1528)

During the Renaissance, the d'Este family, which ruled the city-state of Ferrara, were great patrons of the arts. Ludovico Mazzolino worked at the d'Este court right from the beginning of his career and was noted for the bright, jewel-like colors of his paintings. *The Incredulity of Saint Thomas* illustrates Chapter 20 of the Gospel of Saint John. When Jesus first appeared to the disciples after his resurrection, Thomas was away. Informed of Christ's appearance, Thomas said, "Except I shall see in his hands the print of the nails . . . and thrust my hand into his side, I will not believe." Eight days later, Jesus came again and invited Thomas to "behold my hands; and reach hither thy hand, and thrust it into my side: and be not faithless, but believing."

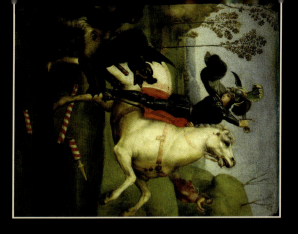

505
Oil on wood
Musée du Louvre, Paris

Saint George and the Dragon
Raphael Sanzio (1483–1520)

Raphael received his first artistic training from his father, a minor painter in the city-state of Urbino. By age 17, he was already being called a master. Raphael moved to Florence in 1504, when Leonardo da Vinci was painting the *Mona Lisa* and Michelangelo had just finished sculpting *David*. The work of both these artists would influence Raphael, who became a master of Leonardo's sfumato technique (the use of very delicate shading to refine forms and features). Later, after seeing Michelangelo's work on the ceiling of the Sistine Chapel, Raphael began to use the human body more expressively. *Saint George and the Dragon* was painted in 1505 when Raphael was 22 years old. Legend has it that villagers terrorized by a dragon appeased it each day with a sheep. After the sheep were gone, they drew human victims by lot. On the day the king's daughter was chosen, Saint George happened to be riding by. Raphael's painting captures the moment when Saint George is about to kill the dragon and save the princess, who can be seen in the background at right.

1538
Oil on canvas
Galleria degli Uffizi, Florence

Venus of Urbino
Titian (ca. 1488–1576)

Titian (born Tiziano Vecellio) studied in Venice under two leading painters of the day. By 1516, he'd become official painter to the Republic and for the rest of his long life, dominated the Venetian art world. Rather than making preliminary drawings, Titian seems to have painted directly on the canvas, using layers of color to model the figures and background. Michelangelo is said to have admired Titian's use of color but criticized his drawing, despite the fact that Titian was an excellent draftsman. Though the painting here is titled *Venus of Urbino*, the young woman pictured may not have been intended to represent the goddess of love. She may simply have been the subject of an erotic painting commissioned by Guidobaldo II della Rovere, the duke of Urbino. Some critics, however, contend that the painting was intended to celebrate della Rovere's marriage in 1534, referring to the sleeping dog, which symbolizes faithfulness, and the two traditional marriage chests in the background. The two women may be servants removing or replacing one of their mistress's gowns.

542–1544
Oil on canvas
Santa Maria della Salute, Venice

David and Goliath
Titian (ca. 1488–1576)

In *David and Goliath*, one of three dramatic ceiling paintings now in the Basilica of Santa Maria della Salute, Titian's muscular figures and expressive use of the human body show the influence of Michelangelo. With the decapitated Goliath lying at his feet, David raises his hands to thank God for his victory. The golden light shining through billowing dark clouds, the foreshortened figures, and the viewpoint from below all serve to heighten the drama of the moment.

Oil on canvas
Museo Civico, Padua

Supper in the House of Simon the Pharisee
Tintoretto (1518–1594)

Born in Venice, Jacopo Robusti was the son of a professional dyer, or *tintore*, which is how he came to be called Tintoretto ("little dyer"). After a brief time in Titian's workshop, Tintoretto determined to teach himself. It's said he had the words "The design of Michelangelo and the color of Titian" inscribed on the wall of his studio, and the energy and expressiveness of his paintings are reminiscent of the two artists' later work. The painting shown here depicts a scene from Chapter 8 of the Gospel of Saint Luke. After Jesus was invited to a meal by Simon the Pharisee, a woman entered the house "weeping, and began to wash [Christ's] feet with tears . . ." Simon points out that the woman "is a sinner." Jesus responds, saying, "Seest thou this woman? I entered into thine house, thou gavest me no water for my feet: but she has washed [them] with tears . . . Wherefore I say unto thee, her sins, which are many, are forgiven."

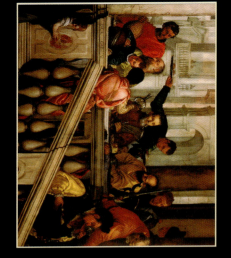

1573
Oil on canvas
Galleria della Accademia, Venice

The Feast in the House of Levi (detail)

Paolo Veronese (1528–1588)

Paolo Caliari learned painting in Verona, the city of his birth and derivation of the name Veronese, but did not reach the peak of his artistic powers until after moving to Venice in 1553. He was noted for his strong colors and complex compositions featuring architectural frameworks and details of everyday life. All those elements can be seen in his immense painting (18 feet 2 inches by 42 feet) originally titled *The Last Supper.* Because of this painting, Veronese was called before the Holy Tribunal of the Inquisition for irreverence and heresy. When he appeared on July 18, 1573, he was asked if it seemed fitting to include "buffoons, drunkards, Germans, [and] dwarfs" and ordered to change the painting within three months. Relieved to have gotten off so easily, Veronese nevertheless ignored the tribunal's instructions and simply renamed the painting *The Feast in the House of Levi.* One of the German soldiers objected to by the tribunal can be seen drinking on the stairs in the lower right corner of the detail shown.

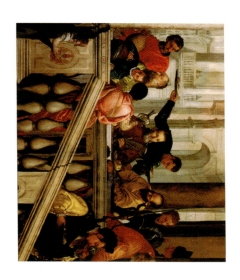

1597–1599
Oil on canvas
Metropolitan Museum of Art, New York

View of Toledo
El Greco (1541–1614)

The artist known as El Greco was born Domenico Theotokopulos in Crete, then a territory of the Republic of Venice. His early training was as a painter of icons in the flat Byzantine style. After moving to Venice in 1567, El Greco studied for a time in Titian's workshop, where he embraced Renaissance painting, learning perspective, anatomy, and how to make a painting tell a story. In 1576, he left Italy for Spain, finally settling in Toledo. It was here that he developed the dramatic expressive style that would make him famous. Among his most celebrated paintings, *View of Toledo* is one of El Greco's two surviving landscapes. It's also one of the first independent landscapes to appear in Western art and, perhaps, one of the most expressive, with its storm-tossed clouds letting just enough moonlight through to bathe the city in an eerie light.

1621-1625
Oil on canvas
Musée du Louvre, Paris

Henry IV Receiving the Portrait of Marie de Médici (detail)
Peter Paul Rubens (1577–1640)

Peter Paul Rubens learned to paint in Antwerp (then part of Flanders, ruled by Spain), where he became a master in the Guild of Saint Luke. In 1601, he left for Italy where he studied the works of the great 15th-century Renaissance masters. After Rubens returned to Antwerp in 1609, he became the most sought-after painter in Flanders, creating works with religious, mythological, and historical themes as well as portraits. To fulfill his many commissions, he established a large workshop. Rubens would make small oil sketches of his proposed paintings, which he used to work out his compositions and secure commissions. His assistants also used them as a guide in producing the large-scale paintings. Rubens would correct their work, complete important areas of the paintings, and add the finishing touches. In 1621, Marie de Médici, widow of France's King Henry IV, commissioned Rubens to personally paint a series of paintings to illustrate her life. In the detail of the painting shown here, Henry IV gazes at the portrait of de Médici, whom he hasn't yet met. The pleased expression on Henry's face, however, leaves little doubt that he'll agree to the arranged marriage.

1628
Oil on canvas
Museo del Prado, Madrid

Saint Cecilia
Nicolas Poussin (1594–1665)

The son of a farmer in Normandy, Nicolas Poussin first studied with minor painters in Paris, however, little is known of his work before he left France for Italy. He apparently spent some time in Venice before traveling to Rome in 1624, where he would live for the rest of his life. A deep interest in Roman antiquities and an admiration for the works of Titian and Raphael led Poussin to develop a classical style instead of painting in the theatrical Baroque style then popular. The influence of Titian's use of color can be seen in Poussin's painting of Saint Cecilia, who was martyred in second- or third-century Rome, where Christianity was illegal. There's no record of her being associated with music until the late 1400s, when she was declared the patron saint of church music. The connection may have come from an old text, which says that while listening to music on her wedding day she was singing a prayer to God to help her keep her vow of chastity. In Poussin's painting, Saint Cecilia is playing the organ while reading sheet music held by two cherubs, as another cherub and two children look on.

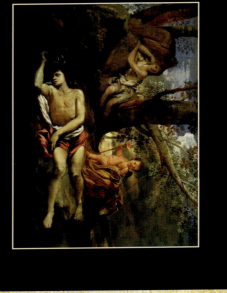

ca. 1629–1630
Oil on canvas
Musée du Louvre, Paris

Echo and Narcissus
Nicolas Poussin (1594–1665)

In the late 1620s, Poussin created a number of mythological paintings drawn from Ovid's *Metamorphoses*. Echo was a nymph who told entertaining stories to distract Juno, the queen of the gods, from the amorous pursuits of her husband, Jupiter. As punishment, Juno took away Echo's ability to speak unless another spoke first. Echo later fell in love with the beautiful youth Narcissus, who spurned her. Distraught, she wandered the woods till nothing was left of her but her voice. Narcissus, who rejected all of his many would-be lovers, eventually received his comeuppance from an avenging goddess. One day, tired and thirsty, he came to a clear, still spring. As he bent over to drink, he saw and fell in love with what he thought was a water spirit—but of course, it was only his own reflection. When he realized he could never possess his love, he pined away and died, and his body turned into the flowers called after him. In the painting, the dead Narcissus lies near the spring, while Cupid and an ethereal Echo keep watch.

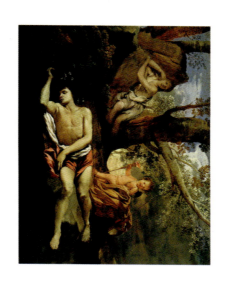

1656
Oil on canvas
Museo del Prado, Madrid

The Maids of Honor
Diego Rodríguez de Silva y Velázquez (1599–1660)

Diego Velázquez received his first artistic training in Seville, the city where he was born. In 1623, he traveled to Madrid, where he painted a portrait of King Philip IV. The king was so taken with this work that he made Velázquez a court painter and said that from then on, he would be the only artist to paint the king's portrait. When Peter Paul Rubens paid a diplomatic visit to Madrid in 1628, he introduced Velázquez to the king's collection of Titian's paintings. Afterward, Titian's influence could be seen in Velázquez's freer brushwork and coloring. Painted toward the end of Velázquez's life, *The Maids of Honor* shows the artist at the peak of his powers. At the center stands the Infanta Margarita, heir to the throne, with a maid of honor on each side. To the left stands Velázquez working on a large canvas, probably painting King Philip IV and Queen Mariana, who can be seen reflected in the mirror in the back of the room. On the walls hang paintings by Rubens.

ca. 1657
Oil on linen
Museo del Prado, Madrid

The Spinners or **The Fable of Arachne** (detail)
Diego Rodríguez de Silva y Velázquez (1599–1660)

Painted the year after *The Maids of Honor* (pages 48–49), *The Spinners* depicts the myth of Arachne from Ovid's *Metamorphoses*. Proud of her great skills as a weaver, Arachne boasted that her work rivaled the weaving of the goddess Athena. When Athena heard this, she visited Arachne disguised as a peasant and warned her that she would be wise not to compare her work to that of the gods. Arachne scoffed at this, challenging Athena to a contest to see who could create the best tapestry. When Arachne's tapestry turned out to be as splendid as Athena's, the goddess lost her temper. She not only destroyed Arachne's tapestry and loom but also caused Arachne to feel so guilty about what she'd done that she hanged herself. At this, Athena felt sorry and turned Arachne into a spider. Velázquez painted a double picture, showing Athena and Arachne as real spinners in the foreground, and as mythological figures in a tapestry in the background. In the detail shown, Athena, disguised as a peasant, sits at her loom. In the background she can be seen in goddess form wearing a helmet.

ca. 1635–1639
Oil on canvas
Gemäldegalerie Alte Meister, Dresden

Rembrandt and Saskia in the Scene of the Prodigal Son in the Tavern

Rembrandt Harmensz van Rijn (1606–1669)

Rembrandt Harmensz van Rijn was born in Leiden, where at age 14, he was enrolled in the university. Uninterested in his lessons, he quit to study art, first in Leiden and then in Amsterdam. His studies over, he returned to Leiden and began teaching at the age of 22. Rembrandt moved to Amsterdam in 1631 and three years later, he married his art dealer's niece, Saskia van Uylenburgh. In this portrait, based on the story of the prodigal son, Saskia sits on Rembrandt's lap as he smiles happily and seemingly toasts the viewer. Despite his artistic success, however, Rembrandt led a less than happy life. Saskia died in 1642 at the age of 30. Of the four sons she bore him, only one survived infancy and even he predeceased his father. Fond of living well, Rembrandt was forced to declare bankruptcy in 1656, though he continued to produce one masterpiece after another. Today, Rembrandt is equally famous for his masterful drawings, paintings, and prints.

1650
Oil on canvas
Museo del Prado, Madrid

Rebecca and Eliezer
Bartolomé Esteban Murillo (1618–1682)

Bartolomé Esteban Murillo spent his whole life in Seville, eventually becoming the city's leading painter. Most of Murillo's paintings had religious themes and show the influence of Diego Velázquez as well as northern European artists such as Peter Paul Rubens. Unlike many religious paintings of the time, Murillo's exhibit a human warmth and sweetness that would be emulated for many years by artists throughout Spain and its colonies in the New World. The painting shown here depicts a scene from Chapter 24 of Genesis. Abraham sent his servant Eliezer to seek a wife for his son Isaac. In the city of Nahor in Mesopotamia, Eliezer waited at a well and said to God, "Let it come to pass that the damsel to whom I shall say, Let down thy pitcher, I pray thee, that I may drink; and she shall say, Drink, and I will give thy camels drink also: let the same be she that thou has appointed for thy servant Isaac." The painting captures the moment Rebecca offers the water to Eliezer.

ca. 1670–1672
Oil on canvas
The National Gallery, London

A Young Woman Seated at a Virginal
Johannes Vermeer (1632–1675)

Johannes Vermeer lived his entire life in Delft, the Netherlands. Little is known about his early training, but his membership in the Guild of Saint Luke, which regulated the sale of paintings in Delft, suggests he spent several years apprenticed to a master painter. Compared to other Dutch painters of his time, Vermeer's output was very low. Of the 45 paintings he is thought to have produced, 34 are known today. Nevertheless, Vermeer is considered to be one of the most accomplished 17th-century Dutch artists. Most of Vermeer's paintings show upper-class domestic interior scenes and are notable for their careful composition, accurate perspective, and naturalistic play of light. In the painting shown, a young woman is playing a virginal, a keyboard instrument shaped like a box on legs. In the background, Vermeer has reproduced a section of *The Procuress*, a painting by Dirck van Baburen.

726
Fresco
Palazzo Patriarcale, Udine

Rachel Hiding the Idols from Her Father (detail)
Giovanni Battista Tiepolo (1696–1770)

Aside from a few years each in Germany and Spain, Giovanni Battista Tiepolo lived in Venice, though he did travel throughout northern Italy painting the illusionistic frescoes for which he is best known. The vivid colors and contemporary architectural elements that appear in his paintings indicate the influence of Paolo Veronese's work. In 1726, Tiepolo went to the remote mountain town of Udine, where he'd been commissioned to paint the ceilings and walls of the Palazzo Patriarcale. Shown is a detail from one of the frescoes in the gallery that illustrates a scene from Chapter 31 of Genesis. When Rachel fled her father Laban's house with Jacob, she stole Laban's idols. Laban pursued and caught up with them. In the painting, she is sitting on the seat where she has hidden the stolen images. The detail pictures servants and children watching as the two confront each other.

1729
Fresco
Palazzo Patriarcale, Udine

Solomon's Decision (detail)
Giovanni Battista Tiepolo (1696–1770)

When Giovanni Battista Tiepolo painted the magnificent frescoes in the Palazzo Patriarcale in Udine, he was assisted by Girolamo Colonna (1688–ca. 1766). Colonna specialized in perspective and throughout the years, would be responsible for painting the architectural elements in Tiepolo's frescoes. *Solomon's Decision* decorated the ceiling of the Palazzo's pink room. The fresco illustrates the famous story about King Solomon from the Old Testament. Two women came before Solomon, both of whom had recently given birth. One woman's child had died, and each claimed the living child was hers and asked Solomon to judge between them. Solomon told his servants to bring a sword and said, "Divide the living child in two, and give half to the one, and half to the other." One of the women agreed to this, but the other one said, "O my lord, give her the living child, and in no wise slay it." By that, Solomon knew her for the true mother and gave her the child. The detail shows Solomon on the left as he orders his servant to divide the child.

ca. 1755
Oil on canvas
Galleria degli Uffizi, Florence

Ducal Palace and the Plaza of Saint Mark's (detail)
Canaletto (1697–1768)

Following in his father's footsteps, Giovanni Antonio Canal (Canaletto means "little canal") first worked as a painter of theatrical scenery in Venice. It was during a visit to Rome when he was in his early twenties that Canaletto decided to quit the theater and devote himself to painting the *vedute* (views) for which he became famous. He was particularly favored by English tourists who bought his cityscapes of Venice to take home as souvenirs. A British merchant and entrepreneur named Joseph Smith collected Canaletto's work and commissioned a group of paintings he later had made into etchings to sell to tourists who couldn't afford an original painting. *Ducal Palace and the Plaza of Saint Mark's* was created the year Canaletto returned to Venice after spending nine years working in England. While Canaletto's paintings show his mastery of perspective and architectural detail (he may have used a camera obscura as an aid), they are enlivened by the inclusion of ordinary people going about their daily business.

1765
Oil on canvas
Gallerie dell'Accademia, Venice

Perspective with Portico
Canaletto (1697–1768)

Canaletto's cityscapes and landscapes were generally accurate though he would occasionally move things around a bit to improve the composition of a painting. He also painted *capricci*, views that were drawn from the imagination but included realistic detail. The *capriccio* shown depicts the portico and courtyard of a palace, where various members of the household go about their work.

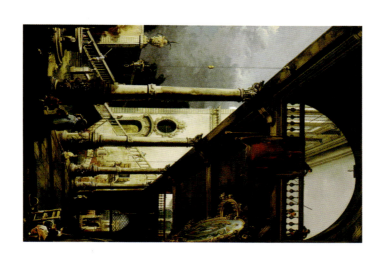

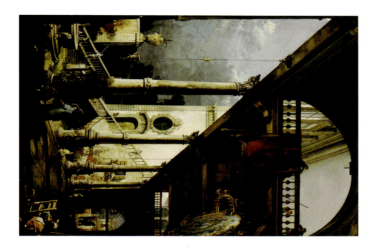

Vespers (detail)
Louis Joseph Watteau (1731–1798)

774
Oil on canvas
Musée des Beaux-Arts, Valenciennes

Louis Joseph Watteau was born in Valenciennes, where he began his studies before moving to Paris. In 1755, he became an instructor at a newly established art school in Lille, a job he lost when his practice of teaching life drawing from the nude caused a scandal. Watteau returned to Valenciennes, where he opened a studio. In 1770, he returned to work in the School of Art in Lille and eight years later, became the headmaster. Watteau also helped found the Academy of Valenciennes and in 1795, started the museum in that city. One of four paintings in Watteau's series called The Four Hours of the Day, *Vespers* pictures a farming family and their workers hurrying to get in the harvest before overtaken by an approaching storm.

767
Oil on canvas
Wallace Collection, London

The Swing
Jean-Honoré Fragonard (1732–1806)

Jean-Honoré Fragonard began his artistic training in Paris at the age of 18. Two years later, he won the Prix de Rome (a scholarship for art students that awarded a four-year stay in Italy), and after three years of training as a history painter, set off for the Académie de France in Rome. During his six years in Italy, Fragonard drew copies of Italian masterworks, sketched the Italian gardens and countryside, and produced small paintings for wealthy collectors. After returning to France, he was admitted to the Royal Academy but soon turned to painting the carefree romantic outdoor scenes for which he is best known. *The Swing*, probably Fragonard's most famous picture, was said to be painted at the behest of a nobleman who wanted a picture of his mistress being pushed on a swing by a bishop while the nobleman was positioned so that he could see up her skirts. The statue of Cupid holding his fingers to his lips cautions the viewer as voyeur to remain quiet and not give away the conspiracy.

1776
Oil on canvas
Museo del Prado, Madrid

Picnic on the Banks of the Manzanares (detail)
Francisco José de Goya y Lucientes (1746–1828)

The son of a gilder in the town of Fuendetodos, Francisco de Goya was apprenticed to an artist in Saragossa before training in Madrid with Francisco Bayeu, a court painter. He married Bayeu's sister Josefa in 1773 and two years later, the couple moved to Madrid. In 1776, Goya was commissioned to create more than 40 cartoons (large paintings that would later be recreated in tapestries of the same size) for two royal palaces. Unfamiliar with the process, his early designs—one of which was *Picnic on the Banks of the Manzanares*—brought complaints from factory officials that the paintings were too filled with detail to reproduced on a loom. It's not known how Goya received this criticism but afterward, he did simplify his designs. In the detail of the painting shown, two young men drink a toast to each other while behind them, a smiling man watches indulgently and a woman sips wine from a glass.

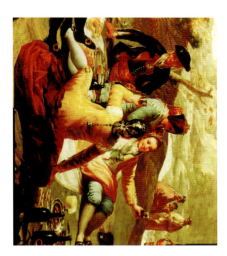

1786-1787
Oil on canvas
Museo del Prado, Madrid

The Flower Girls or Spring
Francisco José de Goya y Lucientes (1746–1828)

In 1783, Francisco de Goya began painting portraits for the nobility, which brought him to the attention of King Charles III. After he was given the position of painter to the king in 1786, Goya painted four tapestry cartoons representing the seasons for the Palacio del Pardo. In *The Flower Girls*, his mastery of the form can be seen in the simplified modeling of the figures and the reduction of the background to a virtual stage set.

1786–1787
Oil on canvas
Museo del Prado, Madrid

The Snowstorm or *Winter*
Francisco José de Goya y Lucientes (1746–1828)

The Snowstorm is one of four tapestry cartoons showing the seasons that Francisco de Goya painted for the Palacio del Pardo. The picture is unusual for a tapestry painting of the time in that it depicts travelers struggling against a storm rather than people enjoying the outdoor pleasures of winter or inside taking comfort in front of a warm fire.

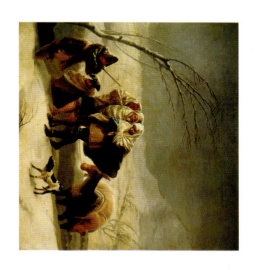

1814
Oil on canvas
Museo del Prado, Madrid

The Third of May 1808
Francisco José de Goya y Lucientes (1746–1828)

Shortly after King Charles IV ascended to the throne in 1789—the same year as the French Revolution—Francisco de Goya was appointed court painter. In 1793, Goya suffered a severe illness that left him deaf. That same year, France declared war and in 1808, Napoleon's armies invaded and conquered Spain. Despite his revulsion at the atrocities committed by the French army, Goya, like many others, declared his allegiance to the new king, Joseph Bonaparte. When Napoleon was forced to abdicate in 1814, Ferdinand VII, the son of Charles IV, gained the throne. Goya was, of course, questioned about his loyalties. He responded with two dramatic paintings, one of them *The Third of May 1808*. In it, Goya shows Spanish rebels being executed by a French firing squad. Despite these two paintings and his series of 85 prints called The Disasters of War that he'd begun as early as 1810, Goya received no commissions from Ferdinand. In 1824, Goya moved to Bordeaux, where he died four years later.

787

Oil on canvas

Musée du Chateau de Versailles

Queen Marie-Antoinette and Her Children

Marie-Louise-Élisabeth Vigée Lebrun (1755–1842)

Marie-Louise-Élisabeth Vigée Lebrun was one of the first two women admitted to the Royal Academy. Her first teacher was her father, a portrait artist who died when she was 12. Within three years, Vigée Lebrun was able to support her family with earnings from her portrait painting. At age 20, she married an art dealer, partly to escape the tyranny of her stepfather. Unfortunately, Lebrun was a gambler who spent her money as well as his own. In 1779, Vigée Lebrun was summoned to paint the first of many portraits of Marie-Antoinette, and the two became friends. *Queen Marie-Antoinette and Her Children* is the last portrait of the queen that Vigée Lebrun painted from life. The empty cradle seen in the background refers to the queen's infant daughter who had died after the painting was begun. At the start of the French Revolution, Vigée Lebrun escaped France and spent the next 12 years traveling throughout Europe. She returned to Paris in 1801 and published her memoirs, *Souvenirs de ma vie*, in 1835 and 1837. By the time she died at age 87, Vigée Lebrun had painted more than 600 portraits and 200 landscapes.

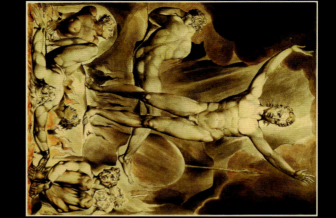

1808
Pen and black ink and watercolor
Victoria and Albert Museum, London

Satan Arousing the Rebel Angels
William Blake (1757–1827)

William Blake was a poet, engraver, and printmaker, who claimed the poems and images he created were revealed to him in visions. He spent about a year at the Royal Academy School in London but left because he felt its teachers repressed imagination and creativity—in his view, like society in general. Blake agreed with the French philosopher Jean-Jacques Rousseau (1712–1778), who believed that people were born inherently good but were eventually corrupted by society. Blake studied manuscript illumination, and in the 1780s, began composing, hand-lettering, illustrating, and publishing books of poems. Today, the most famous of these is *Songs of Innocence*. Blake also created illustrations and prints for scenes from the Bible, Shakepeare, Dante, and John Milton. *Satan Arousing the Rebel Angels* depicts a scene from Milton's epic poem *Paradise Lost*. Throughout his work, Blake is concerned primarily with the human figure, and his admiration for Michelangelo can clearly be seen in his muscular figures.

1838
Oil on canvas
The National Gallery, London

The Fighting Temeraire Tugged to Her Last Berth to Be Broken Up

J. M. W. Turner (1775–1851)

At age 15, Joseph Mallord William Turner exhibited his first painting at the Royal Academy School in London. He began exhibiting at the Academy regularly in 1790, and in 1802, became the youngest artist ever to be elected a full academician. During his early career, Turner traveled the countryside drawing and painting watercolors of the picturesque landscapes and selling the drawings to engravers to support himself. By the 1800s, however, he'd begun developing the style that would make him famous. Now painting in oils, his work combined historical and mythological themes with dramatic atmospheric effects that dominated the paintings, comparing the awesome powers of nature to the seemingly insignificant activity of man. *The Fighting Temeraire* played an important role in the 1805 Battle of Trafalgar, but by the 1830s, sailing ships were being replaced by steamships. In his painting, Turner evokes the end of an era by picturing a ghostly *Temeraire*, its masts empty of sails, being towed by a steam-powered tugboat belching smoke against the setting sun.

ca. 1828-1833
Oil on canvas
Musée du Louvre, Paris

François I, Accompanied by the Queen of Navarre, His Sister, and the Court, Receives Paintings and Statues from Italy by Primaticcio

Alexandre-Evariste Fragonard (1780–1850)

The son of Jean-Honoré Fragonard, Alexandre-Evariste was a child prodigy, beginning his artistic studies with the famed painter Jacques-Louis David at the age of 12 and exhibiting in the Paris Salon for the first time at age 13. Alexandre-Evariste would go on to become not only a painter, but also a sculptor, architect, and book illustrator as well as a costume designer and creator of designs for Sèvres china. He painted in the neoclassical style popular after the French Revolution, a style his father had not been able to adapt to. Given the politically unstable times Alexandre-Evariste lived in, a number of his works were left uncompleted or, in some cases, destroyed. In his late 30s, he began producing historical paintings. The work shown was one of several on the theme of "the history of France and the Arts" commissioned for the ceilings of a gallery in the Louvre.

1866
Oil on paper, stretched on canvas
Musée Fabre, Montpellier

Antiochus and Stratonice
Jean-Auguste-Dominique Ingres (1780–1867)

After leaving the academy in Toulouse, Jean-Auguste-Dominique Ingres moved to Paris to continue his artistic studies in 1796. He won the Prix de Rome in 1801, but his trip to the Académie de France in Italy was delayed until 1806. After his time at the academy was up, Ingres, lacking the recognition in France that he felt his work had earned, decided to remain in Italy. He only returned to France after the painting he exhibited at the 1824 Paris Salon was met with great acclaim. Ingres's greatest strengths were his portraits, especially of women, and his history paintings. The ancient story of Antiochus and Stratonice was one Ingres returned to several times. In the painting, Antiochus, prince of Syria, lies dying of an unknown illness. The doctor has just laid his hand on the prince's heart and realized that the cause of his illness is his forbidden love for his stepmother, Stratonice. The king, to save his son's life, decides to give up his wife so she and Antiochus can marry.

1850
Oil on canvas
Musée d'Orsay, Paris

Morning: Dance of the Nymphs
Jean-Baptiste-Camille Corot (1796–1875)

The son of a successful Paris milliner, Jean-Baptiste-Camille Corot did as he was expected and went into business. This did not suit Corot, however, and at the age of 26, he persuaded his father to support him in his efforts to become an artist. From the very beginning, Corot painted *en plein air* (outdoors), quickly executing small oil sketches that he neither exhibited nor turned into finished paintings. In 1825, Corot traveled to Italy where he spent three years. As before, he worked outside and quickly, however, this time, the small pictures were not sketches but completed works whose colors were so rich, they evoked the heat of the Italian sun. It wasn't until the late 1840s that Corot began to paint in the style for which he is best known. Instead of working directly from nature, he created his landscapes from memory, using feathery brushstrokes and filling the pictures with a soft, silvery light. *Morning: Dance of the Nymphs* calls to mind an idealized countryside where nymphs frolic happily among the trees.

GLOSSARY

altarpiece   A painted or carved artwork consisting of one or more panels placed above and behind the altar of a church.

assemblage   An artwork assembled from various odds and ends, such as paper, cloth, wood, found objects, or junk.

Baroque   An artistic style characterized by the use of extravagant decoration in architecture and colorful, dramatic designs in paintings.

camera obscura   An enclosure or box, the inside of which is entirely dark except for a small opening (which may be fitted with a lens) that admits light, projecting an inverted image on the opposite side.

capriccio (pl. *capricci*)   A landscape view that includes realistic detail but is drawn from the artist's imagination.

cartoon   A large painting created as a pattern for a tapestry.

chiaroscuro   The use of light and shade instead of line to model forms and figures.

city-state   An independent state comprised of a city and its surrounding territory.

classical   Of or relating to the art, architecture, literature, philosophy, and ideals of ancient Rome and Greece.

collage   An artwork made of various cut-up materials glued onto a surface.

engraving   A print produced by using a pointed tool called a burin to cut a design into a metal plate, removing the burr from the edges of the grooves then rubbing ink into them, wiping the excess ink off the surface, covering the plate with a sheet of damp paper, and running it through a press to create an image the reverse of the one on the plate; also, the act or process of making an engraving

foreshorten   A technique used to reduce or distort forms that project or recede from the picture plane in order to make them look three-dimensional.

fresco   An artwork created by painting with water-based pigments on fresh plaster, which absorbs the colors so the picture becomes part of the wall.

genre picture   An artwork that pictures ordinary people in a scene from everyday life.

humanist   During the Renaissance, a person who studied the arts and ideals of ancient Rome and Greece. Humanism came to reflect a belief in the separation of church and state, a well rounded education, and the worth of the individual.

Inquisition   A Roman Catholic tribunal (court) once used to seek out and punish heresy.

linear perspective   A mathematically derived technique that imagines parallel lines converging at a vanishing point on a horizon line in order to create the illusion of three-dimensional space on a two-dimensional surface.

Ovid   A Roman poet who lived from 43 B.C.E. to ca. C.E. 17.

Reformation   The religious movement set in motion when Martin Luther called for reform in the Catholic Church in 1517, which led to the establishment of Protestant religions.

Renaissance   The period lasting from about 1400 to 1650 in Europe that marked the end of the Middle Ages and the beginning of modern times. Brought about by social, political, and economic changes, the Renaissance was a time of intense cultural activity inspired by the Humanistic revival of interest in the arts of ancient Rome and Greece.

Rococo   An artistic style similar to Baroque but with the added element of lighthearted fantasy.

Romanticism   An artistic style, especially in painting, that emphasized imagination and the emotions.

sfumato   The use of very fine shading to model delicate forms and features.

tempera   A type of paint produced by mixing pigments with egg yolk and water.

triptych   A carved or painted picture on a three-piece panel with hinged sides.

woodcut   A handmade print made by pressing paper onto an inked block of wood in which lettering, a design, or an image has been created by cutting away the areas that are not to print.

INDEX

IMAGE CREDITS